OWL BE SEEING YOU
(A Grumpy the Iguana and Green Parrot Adventure)

By: Susan Marie Chapman

Illustrated by: Natalia Loseva

To my son, Michael.
My biggest fan.

Published 2022

Printed in the United States of America
Print ISBN: 978-1-7368056-3-3

Canoe Tree Press
4697 Main Street
Manchester, VT 05255
www.CanoeTreePress.com

Grumpy was fast asleep in his cozy little iguana bed dreaming of Grumpy snacks.

Suddenly he was awakened by a loud noise.

"*What was that,*" thought Grumpy, as he made his way outside to investigate.

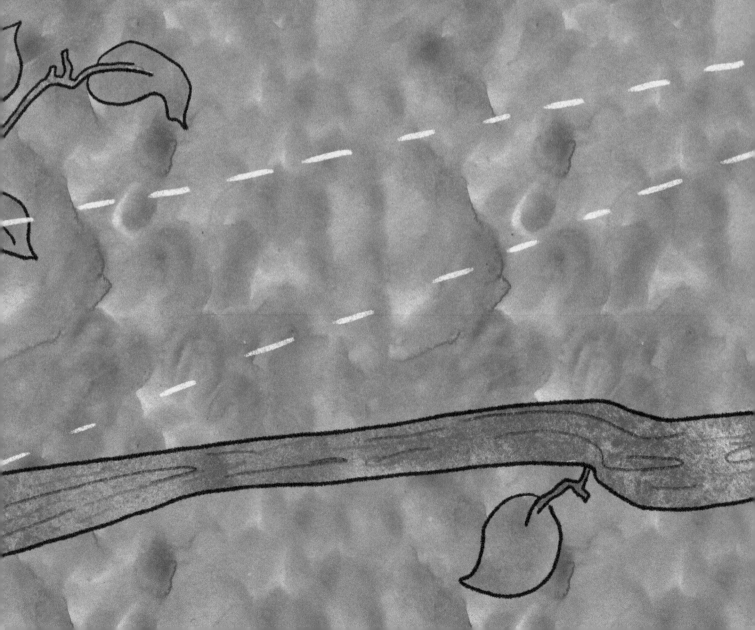

On a branch high above Flamingo Park, a young screech owl sat. He was scanning the park with laser sharp focus, searching for something or someone.

The screech owl looked up at the moon and called out with a loud whinny (like the sound a horse makes). The sound was so loud that Grumpy nearly fall out of his tree.

"There is that sound again," thought Grumpy.

As he looked up into the night sky, he noticed an owl. "Is that you making all that noise?" Grumpy asked.

"We met exactly one year ago and made a promise to meet up again tonight."

Screech Owl looked up at the full moon and whinnied as loud as he could.
"Where are you my sweetheart? I miss you."

Grumpy put his hands over his ears.
Wow, these owls sure are loud.

"Can you please try to use your quiet voice. I need to get some sleep," Grumpy said, as he stepped into his tree home and closed the door.

Screech Owl started to cry.
Where are you my sweetheart? I miss you.

Screech owls are small rust colored owls who stand about 8 inches tall (the same size as a robin).

Screech Owls have big yellow eyes.

They have very pronounced ear tufts that point straight up when they are listening intently to something.

Owls have amazing eyesight. They can spot a mole from two miles away in the sky. It is like looking through a pair of binaculars for us.

Screech Owl flew to the other side of the park to see if his sweetheart was there. He certainly did not want to wake Grumpy up again, he thought, as he glided silently through the sky.

Screech Owl noticed an abandoned woodpecker home in an old tree trunk as he reached his destinaton.

He quickly flew inside and tucked himself in. He was now instantly camouflaged from predators. Screech looked up at the moon as he waited for his sweetheart.

Grumpy had just fallen back to sleep again. His best friend and roommate, the Green Parrot, was away visiting family on Key Biscayne Island. Grumpy had the whole tree house to himself and he was enjoying it.

He had a smile on his face knowing that he was not going to be disturbed. Suddenly, he heard that awful screeching sound again. Grumpy mumbled under his breath as he jumped out of bed and marched outside.

He was about to give
Screech Owl a piece of
his mind for disrupting
his sleep again, when
he stopped in his
tracks. This was not
Screech Owl. This was
a totally different owl.
Grumpy rubbed his eyes
and looked again.

What he witnessed was the most beautiful girl owl he had ever seen. She was a little taller than Screech and had big yellow eyes with long eyelashes that you especially noticed when she blinked.

Grumpy also caught sight of a shiny gold feather behind her left ear that sparkled in the moonlight. Her body was a mix of amber and reddish-brown colors similar to Screech Owl's.

Grumpy was confused. "You're not Screech Owl," he stuttered. "I'm Miss Screech Owl and I'm waiting for someone," she said.

"Have you seen him? His name is Screech Owl, and I am his sweetheart."

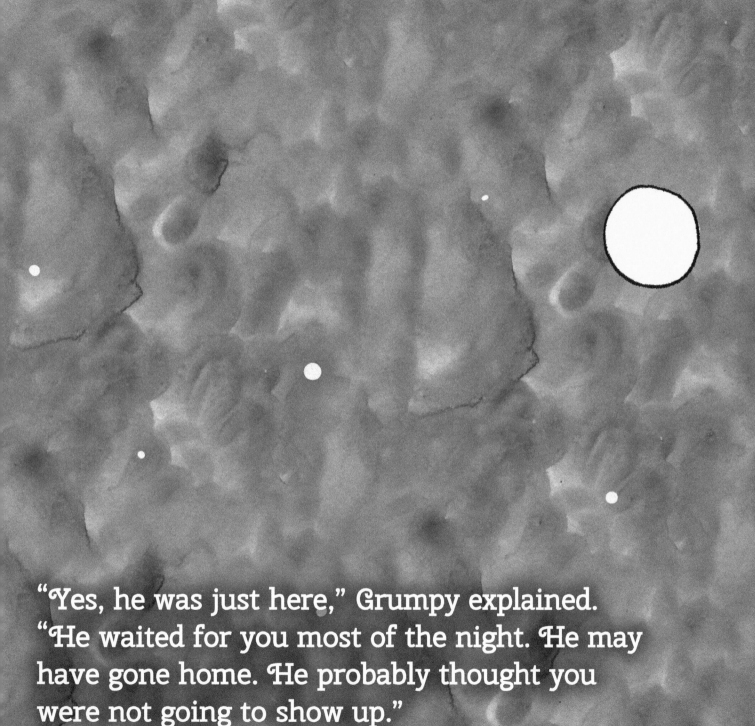

"Yes, he was just here," Grumpy explained. "He waited for you most of the night. He may have gone home. He probably thought you were not going to show up."

Miss Screech Owl let out a shrill cry. "Screech, where are you my love?" Grumpy put his hands over his ears once again. Am I ever going to get any sleep tonight? Grumpy thought to himself.

"He said he would wait for me," Miss Screech Owl said, brokenhearted. She started to cry. "I am truly sorry," Grumpy said.

Miss Screech Owl hung her head and started sobbing uncontrollably. Grumpy ran inside his tree home and grabbed a tissue box to give to the little Owl.

"I would have been here sooner,
but I was followed by a big black cat."

Grumpy burst into laughter. "What's so funny?"
Miss Screech asked.
"The Big Black Cat is my friend and cannot harm
you. He has no teeth and besides he is a vegetarian,"
Grumpy answered.

"Now what should I do?" Miss Screech Owl hooted. "I'm not sure," Grumpy replied. "Maybe you should just go home and come back here again next year."

"I don't want to wait another year to see my Screech Owl," she cried. "Screech's last words to me before he left were; I'll be seeing you, my sweetheart. No matter what I do or where I go, you will always be right here in my heart."

"I know that he would never leave unless he was absolutely sure that I was not going to show up," Miss Owl said. "April is a special month for owls. It's the time of year that young owls choose a mate for life."

"But, I guess you are right, Grumpy, I should just go home." Miss Owl said, as she hung her head in defeat.

"You are home," said a voice high above the trees.

Miss Screech Owl and Grumpy looked up to see Screech coming towards them. "How long have you been up there?" Grumpy asked. "Long enough to know that my sweetheart belongs here with me in Flamingo Park. You are my destiny, my future and my forever sweetheart," Screech Owl said, as he slowly made his way down the tree.

Screech Owl hopped from branch to branch until he was finally sitting next to his sweetheart. They put their heads together and closed their eyes.

Grumpy rolled his eyes.
Kids, he said to himself as
he walked into his tree home
unnoticed and gently closed
the door.

Although Grumpy did not say it, he was very happy for the screech owl addition to Flamingo Park. In fact, Grumpy kinda liked the idea of becoming "Uncle Grumpy" someday. Grumpy smiled as he closed his eyes and fell fast asleep for the third and final time.

THE END

9 781736 805633